Le Havre-
New York

Christian Clères

Le Havre-New York

Translated from the French
by David Britt

POCKET  ARCHIVES
HAZAN

All the documents reproduced in this work come from the collections of the French Lines Association, created in 1995 in order to ensure the unity and the perpetuity of the Compagnie Générale Maritime et Financière's historic patrimony, covering one hundred and fifty years of national maritime history.
The Compagnie Générale Maritime et Financière took over from the Compagnie Générale Transatlantique et des Messageries Maritimes.

Immeuble CGM
22, quai Galliéni
92158 Suresnes Cedex
Tel. : 33 1 46 25 75 89

Avenue Lucien-Corbeaux, BP CGM
76096, Le Havre Cedex
Tel. : 33 2 35 24 19 13

© Éditions Hazan, Paris, 1997
© Association French Lines
  for all the illustrative material
Editor: Éric Reinhardt
Design: Atalante
Production: Muriel Landsperger
Color separation: Seleoffset, Torino
Printing: Milanostampa, Farigliano

ISBN: 2 85025 585 8
ISSN : 1275-5923
Printed in Italy

Contents

A Century of Atlantic Crossings
7

Before the First World War
52

The *Paris*
83

The *Île-de-France*
97

The 1930's and the *Normandie*
115

After the Second World War and the *France*
171

A Century of Atlantic Crossings

Ever since the day when, in his search for a route to the Indies, the Genoese navigator Christopher Columbus came upon a *Terra Incognita*, the new continent has never lost its fascination for the inhabitants of Old Europe. For them, the land that would come to be called America, has always appeared as a place unburdened by the past and promising a better future. The year 1492 marks the onset of a stormy and fascinating chapter in human and maritime history: a record of hope, of laughter, of cool courage, of technological progress and of patriotic pride; a tale of drama and grief, shipwreck and adversity, anguish and disillusion.

When the rush to the New World began, a modest sailing ship – in the wake of the celebrated *Mayflower*, which sailed from Plymouth on September 16, 1620 – would take more than seventy days to cross the North

Atlantic. Two centuries later, the fastest of the clippers linked the continents in thirty-three days westbound and just twenty-five on the eastward run from America to Europe. Under sail, those ships really "clipped" through the waves; but they carried very few passengers. The biggest five-master ever built, the *France II*, shipped just seven.

The first steam engine was built by a Frenchman, Denis Papin, as early as 1690; but it was not until 1819 that an American vessel, the *Savannah*, first crossed the ocean "with auxiliary steam power." (She made the second half of the eastbound crossing under sail, to save on coal.) After thirty-five days at sea, the *Savannah* made a triumphal entry into the port of Liverpool before setting out on the return crossing, which took no less than fifty days.

In 1838, the first regular steamship service to the American continent was inaugurated by two British paddle steamers, the *Sirius* and *Great Western*. The latter sailed from Bristol on April 8, 1838 and reached New York in 15 days 10 hours with sixty or so passengers on board. Two years later, Samuel Cunard set up the British & North American Royal Mail Steam Packet Company (which became the Cunard Company in 1875). Its rapid success inspired an American rival, the Ocean Steamship Company, to start a regular service of its own with the *United States*, a 2,000-ton ship that could carry 1,000 tons of freight. For many years, this was the only transatlantic steamer to call at Le Havre.

While trade between the United States and Europe was booming, France remained out in the cold. True, in the years after France's recognition of U.S. independence, Louis XVI had considered setting up a commercial shipping line to ply between the two countries. But at that date (1783) the King of France had too much else on his mind to take any great interest in far-off America. Emperor Napoleon I revived the idea in 1811, but it was not until the reign of King Louis-Philippe (1830-48) that a French government finally decided to set up a mail service between France and the U.S.

The time was ripe. Dramatic changes were afoot in Europe. In Ireland, Holland and Germany, a terrible famine caused by potato blight forced tens of thousands of people off the land; and they made their way to Liverpool to take ship for the New World. The future importance of sea transport impressed itself on two shipowners of Le Havre, Héroult and de Handel by name, who founded the Compagnie des Paquebots Transatlantiques in 1847. Their company collapsed two years later – at the very time when, after the German-born pioneer John Augustus Sutter struck gold on the Coome River, Americans were rushing to the West Coast in their thousands.

In 1856 the two Gaulthier brothers, from Lyon, threw their hats into the ring by setting up the Compagnie Franco Américaine; but they enjoyed no more success than their predecessors. Louis-Philippe had meanwhile been succeeded by Napoleon III, and he had issued a decree (dated May 2, 1855) authorizing the creation of another shipping line, the Compagnie Générale Maritime. Its principal shareholders were two brothers, disciples of the social philosophy of the Comte de Saint-Simon. Emile and Isaac Pereire had already founded a bank, the Crédit Mobilier, and had helped to set up the first French railroad, from Paris to Saint-Germain-en-Laye. No sooner was the Compagnie Générale Maritime in business than it took over La Terre-Neuvienne, a company founded at Granville in Normandy by Jacques Lecampion and François Théroulde to fish cod on the Newfoundland Banks. On August 25, 1861, having signed its first postal convention with the French State, the Pereires' company became the Compagnie Générale Transatlantique: *la Transat*, later known in English as the French Line.

Within three years, and in return for an annual subsidy of 9.3 million francs, the company undertook to field eleven steamships, five of them on the New York run alone. Orders were placed with the John Scott shipyard at Greenock in Scotland for the steamers *Washington, Lafayette* and *Europe* – and later also for the *Napoléon III, Pereire* and *Ville de Paris*. Obliged by contract to have their five other vessels built in France, Isaac and Emile Pereire dismissed the prices quoted as excessive and set up a shipyard of their own at Penhoët, near Saint-Nazaire. Saint-Nazaire was the port from which ships were already plying to the West Indies – and also to Mexico, where a war was in progress. Napoleon III put pressure on the French Line to ship reinforcements across to help his beleaguered friend, Emperor Maximilian.

Meanwhile, north of the border, the Civil War broke out between the northern and southern United States. Such was the troubled climate in which the first regular steamship service from Le Havre to New York began.

At high tide, 6 p.m., on June 15, 1864, the *Washington*, the first steamer delivered from the Scottish shipyards, proudly hoisted her colors: the mail pennant at the bow, the Stars and Stripes on the foremast, the company's house flag on the mizzenmast, and, at the stern, the tricolor of France. Captain Duchesne was in command. Le Havre was *en fête*. All over the wharves, as far as Frascati beach, an enthusiastic crowd admired the great ship, ironclad throughout, 105 meters (345 feet) long, and propelled by a single steam engine driving two paddle wheels. She was also rigged to proceed under sail, in case of a mechanical breakdown. Amid the name-less throng were a number of dignitaries who had come down from Paris by special train; they included the U.S. Ambassador to France and the French Postmaster-General, who delivered a high-flown eulogy of "the national and Christian work of these new shipping lines, which carry the ideas of religion and of economics to the Far East and to the New World, serving at one and the same time the disinterested apostles of the Gospel and the adventurous missionaries of industry – who in both cases are the pioneers of French civilization."
On board the *Washington*, her sixty-seven passengers (including M. de la Roncière, serving French Ambassador

to the United States) discovered, to their delight, the comforts of life on board: a small lounge decorated in white and gold; lounges with movable tables; a smoking room; two bathrooms; and – the ultimate in comfort – cabins with flush cisterns and tip-up bowls! All this, for 700 francs in first class and 400 francs in second; the less fortunate made the crossing in steerage. After calling in at Brest, the *Washington* reached her mooring at Pier No. 50 in New York just 13 days and 12 hours later, on the morning of June 29, 1864. At the foot of the gangway, the first arrivals were warmly welcomed by George Mackenzie, manager of the French Line's New York office.

Hardly had the French Line gained its toehold in the port of New York when the U.S. Congress voted an increase in tariffs on goods from Europe. The volume of U.S. imports had already dropped markedly over the past three years (177 million francs in 1863, as against 657 million in 1860). Despite this new tariff barrier, the French Line had faith in its future. Equipped with the latest screw propulsion system, the steamers *Impératrice Eugénie*, *Napoléon III*, *Le France*, and *Pereire* linked Le Havre with New York in just nine days, at an average speed of 13 knots. Results over the first few months were so satisfactory that the number of sailings to New York was doubled, from monthly to semimonthly.

The transatlantic link was a flourishing one – until June 12, 1866, the date on which a new law (a French one this time) abolished the protectionist regime set up in the seventeenth century by Louis XIV's minister Jean-Baptiste

Colbert. All tonnage duties and flag surcharges imposed on foreign vessels on entry into French ports were abolished – and the door was thrown open to for-eign, and notably German, competition. Troubles never come singly, and the Pereire brothers were obliged to file for bankruptcy on behalf of the Crédit Mobilier, which had been the principal source of finance for the French Line. On June 28, 1868 they resigned from the board of the shipping line that they themselves had created. These financial hardships were aggravated by the Franco-Prussian War of 1870. Not only were transatlantic mail services reduced to a single monthly crossing but, when the port of Le Havre came under threat as a result of the Prussian occupation of Rouen, the French Line's ships were reduced to sailing (the ultimate disgrace) from the rival English port of Southampton.

The worst was yet to come. At about 2 a.m. on November 22, 1873 the *Ville du Havre* (formerly *Napoléon III*) was rammed on the starboard beam by the ironclad sailing ship *Loch Earn* 1,800 nautical miles from the French coast. The impact was terrible. The cracking of the vessel's bows woke her passengers from their sleep. In just ten minutes, one of the largest and finest French transatlantic liners of the day, 128.5 meters (422 feet) long and recently refitted and enlarged, sank to the bottom, taking with her 226 wretched victims (the American sailing ship *Trimountain*, which came to the rescue, nev-ertheless succeeded in saving 88 lives). After nine years on the North Atlantic run, the French Line had had its first maritime disaster. It was be the first of many.

The company seemed to be dogged by ill-fortune. Six months later, the crew of the *Europe* abandoned ship with six meters (20 feet) of water in the hold. Twelve days after that, the *Amérique* was caught in a storm off Ouessant. Convinced that she was about to sink, her officers panicked and gave the order to abandon ship. Several days later, a sarcastic telegram announced that *Amérique* awaited her owners in Plymouth, England – to which she had been towed, undamaged, by two British ships! The consequences of this *débâcle* were catastrophic. The gibes of the British mariners were soon followed by a loss of confidence on the part of the traveling public.

The year 1875 was marked by the death of the founder and former president of the French Line, Emile Pereire, and by the return of the Pereire family to the company. Isaac brought in his nephew Emile, his son Eugène, who became president, and his son-in-law Salomon Halfon. The new management at once decided to modernize the fleet, first equipping all of its steamers with an electric signal lamp that carried for more than ten miles, and then – a great novelty – using carrier pigeons to maintain the closest possible contact with *terra firma*. Their efforts bore fruit: in March 1876 the *Amérique* made a memorable entry into Plymouth harbor, effacing the shameful memory of the events of 1874; and, between 1875 and 1880, the annual passenger figures doubled from 7,618 to 15,226.

But the company's fleet was aging. Ships like the *Labrador* seemed old-fashioned in comparison with their foreign competitors, which grew ever larger, faster and more luxurious. Furthermore, uncertainty as to the renewal of the postal convention, due to expire in 1883, inclined the management toward caution. For the period up to 1885, the French Line therefore decided to order just one new steamer. But what a steamer that was!

Initially named *Ville de New York*, she finally bore the name of *La Normandie*. She was 140 meters (460 feet) long, 6,000 gross tons, with engines developing 7,000 horsepower, and in sea trials she reached a speed of 17 knots. *La Normandie* had accommodation for 1,047 passengers, of whom 157 were in airy, comfortable, first-class cabins. She was also the first ship to be lit by electricity throughout and the first to possess promenade decks. British-built at Barrow-in-Furness in Lancashire, *La Normandie* cost 6 million francs.

La Normandie was launched in May 1883, and one month later the New York mail convention was renewed for a term of sixteen years from July 22, 1885. In return for an increase of 1.836 million francs in its annual subsidy, the French Line was to build four new steamers in three years. Two of these, *La Bretagne* and *La Champagne*, were ordered from Penhoët; the others, *La Gascogne* and *La Bourgogne*, were built by Chantiers de la Méditerranée at La Seyne-sur-Mer, near Toulon.

These new French liners were an immediate success. Passengers appreciated their graceful lines, with twin funnels and four pole masts rigged with sails. Every cabin had unlimited running water and tip-up bowls. The decor was sumptuous. The furniture was made of rare woods inlaid with chased metal, cameos and onyx; the drapes were plush and satin, with tassels and pompons. Meals on board were of the choicest: the daily menus included soups, hors d'œuvre, salmon *sauce vénitienne*, roast haunch of venison *Grand Veneur*, fillet of beef *Génoise* with green peas and mushrooms, turkey with truffles, and saddle of lamb.

These ships were comfortable, but above all they were fast. *La Bourgogne* made her maiden crossing in 7 days, 13 hours, 45 minutes. *La Bretagne* beat the speed record between Le Havre and New York with an average speed of 19.60 knots. These results earned the French Line the top place in the U.S. Postmaster General's annual listings, and consequently the lucrative European contract for the U.S. Mail. This was a welcome boost to the company, for rivalry was keen on the New York run. In that year, 1886, no less than 151 steamers belonging to 17 different lines called at the port of New York and made 1,317 crossings: more than 25 every week in each direction. The new vessels ordered by Cunard, White Star and the Hamburg-Amerika Line, as well as by American and Italian companies, spurred ambitions all round – ambitions that were fed, from 1880 onward, by an enormous growth in migration to America.
The new nation, declared George Washington on Thanksgiving Day 1795, would become a safe haven for

the wretched of every land. He little knew how right he was. From 1815 through 1860, the United States of America took in more than five million foreign immigrants. After the Irish, the British, the Poles and the Scandinavians, it was the turn of the Germans, then the Austrians, and then (after the murder of Czar Alexander II in 1881) the Russians. Then came the peoples of the Balkans, Greeks made anxious by Turkish expansionism, Christian Armenians menaced by the Muslims, Russian Jews fleeing the pogroms, Sicilians, and finally mainland Italians. Between 1880 and the eve of World War I more than twenty million immigrants landed in the U.S..

For the shipping companies, this human cargo represented a major financial windfall. The British company, Cunard, shipped emigrants from Ireland through Liverpool. In Hamburg and Bremen, the German lines collected those from Central Europe. The Red Star Line of Antwerp shipped emigrants from Switzerland and Germany. The French Line, too, took the situation in hand.

Less well placed geographically than its rivals, and hampered by the exorbitant fares charged by French railway companies, the French Line decided to collect its potential customers from their countries of origin. From 1883 onward, special trains, the *Transat trains*, ran across France from Basel and from Modane, carrying passengers from Switzerland, Germany, Alsace, Austria, and Italy. Travelers were conveyed directly to Le Havre at a modest fare and in tolerable comfort, with twice daily distributions of free coffee as well as milk for children.

Arriving in France's "Ocean City" after more than twenty hours on the train, the future immigrants were shepherded into the French Line's "Transatlantic Tent" (which was replaced in 1906 by a maritime rail terminal). There, they were examined by three doctors in succession. The first examined them all over and vaccinated them; the second examined them all over, again, and looked at the insides of their eyelids; the third examined them all over, yet again, and checked their heads and scalps. The prospect of having to pay the cost of returning any immigrant rejected in New York, plus a hefty fine imposed by the U.S. Administration – not to mention the risk of infection on board ship – led the company to weed out any suspect case right away. As soon as any doubt arose as to an individual's state of health, he or she was taken aside and examined all over again. Any unfortunate who failed to pass muster was confined in a barred pen to await the return of his or her papers before being set at liberty.

The fortunate elect embarked at once and were taken down to the steerage, where they had two-tier bunks arranged one against the next. The vast sleeping areas were located above the engine room, and the noise was unrelenting. The smells were loathsome, the toilets vile, and the overcrowding hard to bear. Separated from passengers in other classes throughout the voyage (and with access only to the promenade deck), the immigrants lived where they slept, eating at wooden tables set up between the bunks. Coffee in the morning; for lunch and for dinner a quarter-liter of wine, soup, beef, vegetables, and dessert. The food was plentiful and good; the reputation of the French Line was at stake.

After eight days at sea, the immigrants at last sighted New York and the promised land of their dreams. But the voyage was not over yet; they still had to pass through the immigration checks on Ellis Island, which was – as Stephen Graham wrote in 1913 – the earthly experience closest to the Last Judgment, the moment when one must prove one's worth before entering Paradise. Opened in 1892 to replace the old Castle Garden Reception Center, Ellis Island lies in the waters of New York harbor, just behind Frédéric Bartholdi's Statue of Liberty (a gift from France in 1885). All third-class immigrants, without exception, were brought here by steam tenders direct from the French Line wharf. The great hall, which holds five thousand people, was constantly full, and the U.S. Immigration Service was constantly stretched to the limit, working night and day, all year round, to cope with the ever-growing numbers of new arrivals. Between 1880 and 1890 the new immigrant population grew from 14 to 22 million. And – after a slowdown during the 1890s caused by a cholera epidemic in Europe and an economic crisis in North America – immigration broke new records from 1900 onward. There were 1,285,349 admissions to U.S. territory in 1907 alone; on April 17 of that year, Ellis Island processed a record total of 11,747 immigrants.

Like all of the other European transatlantic lines, the French Line made big profits from this flow of immigrants, and the future looked so rosy that the company ordered two single-class ships, the *Chicago* and the *Rochambeau*, each with capacity for more than 1,200 immigrants. A few years later, the French Line built its own accommodation center in Le Havre, the 1,000-bed Hôtel des Emigrants on Rue de Phalsbourg.

The turn of the century saw the steerage decks of French liners crowded with immigrants, but first-class passengers were few and far between. The difficulty here was that in 1897 the crew of the *Ville de Saint-Nazaire* had abandoned ship, passengers and crew had drifted in lifeboats for six days, and there had been just seventeen survivors. The French Line stood accused of neglecting the maintenance of its ships, and of keeping them at sea too long: built in 1871, the *Ville de Saint-Nazaire* was twenty-six years old when she was lost.

The chapter of accidents continued. Sixteen months later, on July 4, 1898, another French Line vessel, *La Bourgogne*, collided in fog with the British four-master *Cromartyshire*. There were 565 fatalities. In the noblest seafaring tradition, Captain Deloncle and his senior officers went down with their ship. Despite the courage and self-sacrifice of these men, the ensuing campaign of denigration considerably weakened the French Line. The company returned to favor only in 1906, when its new liner *La Provence* entered service. Here, the great attraction to foreign passengers was not so much the ship's elegant lines, or even the average speed of 21.63 knots that made her one of the five fastest ships in the world, but her long-distance wireless telegraphy station. Wireless telegraphy, with relay transmitters at Poldhu on the European side and Cape Cod in the U.S., permitted *La Provence* to remain in direct contact with the shore throughout the voyage. The French Line took advantage of this exclusive technological breakthrough to publish *L'Atlantique*, a daily newspaper printed on board, which carried the news of the day as received from France and from the U.S.

Meanwhile, in Britain, Cunard brought into service two new liners, both 240 meters (790 feet) long and 32,000 tons gross: the *Mauretania* and the *Lusitania*. These were the largest liners in the world, and also – thanks to their four Parsons turbines – the fastest. They took from their German rivals the famous Blue Ribbon, awarded to the ship that made the fastest crossing between the Bishop Rock and Ambrose lighthouses. In October 1907, the *Lusitania* crossed the Atlantic in 4 days, 19 hours, 52 minutes, at an average speed of 23.99 knots. The *Mauretania* equaled this record one month later and the two English liners sparred for the famous trophy until 1915. It was then that a German submarine, without warning, torpedoed the *Lusitania* and her passengers. The *Mauretania* was to hold the coveted Blue Ribbon for more than twenty years, losing it only in July 1929 to the German liner *Bremen*.

While British and German shipping lines contended for the Blue Ribbon, Charles Roux (who had succeeded Eugène Pereire as president of the French Line in 1904) decided to put the emphasis on the quality of life on board. So he ordered from the Penhoët shipyard a new ship with eight decks, five of which were continuous from stem to stern, and with (for the first time) a promenade deck entirely protected by sliding panes of glass and therefore usable in all weathers. This new liner, the *France* (with four funnels, like her main rivals), could transport a record total of 2,516 people, of whom 1,885 were passengers and 631 crew.

The *France*'s main attraction was the opulence of her interiors. Nothing like it had ever been seen before: the first-class lounge, the Grand Salon, had a ceiling supported by eight columns and lit by a wide skylight and six half-domes; the dining saloon was 8 meters (26 feet) high and rose through three decks, with a staircase modeled on those of the French classical architect Robert de Cotte; the ship's grand staircase reproduced that of the French National Library (the Bibliothèque Nationale). Two large paintings by Lacroix de Marseille dominated the Grand Salon, and all the furnishings were in the Louis Quatorze, Louis Quinze or Regency styles. On April 12 and 13, 1912, the *France* underwent sea trials off Douarnenez and Les Glénans; she was scheduled to sail on her maiden voyage from the Quai de l'Escale in Le Havre one week later. "Rolls well, fast ship," the seamen said of her.

At the same time, across the English Channel, the White Star Line was also preparing for a big event. On April 10, 1912, its latest liner sailed from Southampton for New York on her maiden voyage. Sir Bruce Ismay, the Chairman of White Star, was on board. On the bridge was Captain E. Smith, with just one idea in his head: to steal a march on the rival Cunard Line by capturing the Blue Ribbon from the *Mauretania*. To achieve this, he had decided to set the most northerly course, one that no skipper ever normally chose at that time of year because of the presence of numerous drifting icebergs. But, with her sixteen watertight compartments, Captain Smith's vessel was regarded as unsinkable. Or rather, as corrected in the message transmitted (too late) by the young telegraph operator M. G. Phillips, "practically unsinkable."

On the evening of April 10, the British liner, with 2,358 passengers on board, called in at Cherbourg before setting off to meet her fate. On April 12, at approximately 7:45 p.m., the ocean giant passed *La Touraine*, on her way back from New York, and the French liner signaled a warning of icebergs at approximately 50° West longitude. Captain Smith held his course. On the night of Sunday, April 14, at 10:25 p.m. (about 2 a.m., Paris time), the wireless operator on Cape Race received an alarming message from the British liner: "Have struck an iceberg. We are badly damaged. Titanic. Position 41°44'N., 50°24'W." On board the *Titanic*, the fun continued unabated. None of the passengers was aware of the impending drama.

On Saturday, 20 April, 1912, just five days after the tragic wreck of the *Titanic* and the loss of 1,490 lives, the *France* was preparing for her first transatlantic voyage. To forestall panic among the passengers, the French Line announced in its publicity material that this was "the first ship to have as many places in her lifeboats as there are passengers on board." From that maiden voyage onwards, the *France* was a resounding success. As intended, her sumptuous decor attracted – and delighted – a millionaire clientele. The *France* was promptly dubbed "the Versailles of the Atlantic." Such was the enthusiasm among her American passengers that luxury berths for certain crossings in high seasons were actually sold by auction! Some passengers paid as much as 300,000 francs (at values then current) for the privilege of occupying them for just one crossing. With the *France* (and after the loss of the *Titanic*, which marked a severe setback for the British competition), the French Line was confident of having secured its rightful position on the North Atlantic run: the leading position.

The euphoria did not last. On June 28, 1914, Archduke Franz Ferdinand was murdered in Sarajevo, and the whole of Europe began to slide into war. On August 5, all shipping was confined to port. However, to evacuate the American tourists who would otherwise have been stranded in France, the French government allowed the *France*, with 2,500 passengers, plus the *Rochambeau* and the *Chicago*, to sail from Le Havre. As soon as they returned from New York, these and most other passenger ships were requisitioned and converted into armed merchant cruisers, liners, troopships or hospital ships. Armed vessels of the French Line took part in the landings at the Dardanelles in 1915. On February 26, 1916, *La Provence* was sunk en route for Salonica with 1,698 men of the Third Colonial Regiment on board. As for the

France, she was first transformed into a troopship sailing between Toulon and the Dardanelles. Then she became a hospital ship on the Toulon-Algiers-Salonica route. In April 1917, when the United States entered the war, she was, once again, turned into a troopship ferrying soldiers between New York and Bordeaux.

That war, which everyone expected to be brief and sparing of human life, was to last fifty-two endless months. With the armistice signed at last, the French Line took stock. It had lost thirty ships, one-quarter of its fleet. The *France* was soon back on the New York run, but most of the company's ships were worn out. It had received from the Allies, as prizes of war, just three modest steamers: two of around 7,000 tons gross and another of 4,500 tons, which were renamed *La Bourdonnais*, *Roussillon* and *Macoris*. Fortunately, the *Paris*, the largest French ocean liner ever built to that time, with eleven decks, a length of 234 meters (768 feet), and a gross displacement of 37,000 tons, was still under construction at Penhoët. Left on the stocks throughout the war, she was delivered only in May 1921.

The *Paris* was worth waiting for. From the moment she entered service, she confirmed and enhanced the French Line's reputation. Her decor was resolutely modern and her internal architecture resembled that of the great Parisian department stores. The dining saloon, which rose through three decks, was lit by an impressive glass ceiling with domes. The wrought-iron staircase to the surrounding balcony was adorned with motifs taken from the fables of La Fontaine. A purpose-built auditorium was set aside for movie shows, and the lounge included, as a supreme luxury, a dance floor lit from beneath. The *Paris* had all it took – except that, by the time she first berthed at the French Line pier in New York in June 1921, the U.S. was passing through an unprecedented crisis. With three million unemployed, the country could no longer handle the floods of immigrants who left the Slav countries and Central Europe in the wake of the Russian Revolution of October 1917. In one year, 1920, the French Line alone had transported nearly 55,000 immigrants; the totals forecast for succeeding years were even higher.

It was all too much. The U.S. decided to call a halt to mass immigration. Swiftly, the Harding Act was passed, limiting annual admissions to 357,000 (one-quarter of the previous total); the Johnson Act of 1924 reduced the quota still further to 161,500. The French Line, along with all other European shipping companies, saw its receipts drop sharply (from 235 million francs in 1920 to 87 million in 1923).

The rich pickings afforded by mass immigration were over; but a new clientele – wealthier, more prestigious and more cultivated – was ready to come aboard. It was the 1920s and France was fashionable. In the U.S. every young lady of good family was expected to attend a French finishing school. For Americans, Paris was the center of the world – the world, that is, of parties, the Folies-Bergère, beauty, culture, luxury, refinement and liberty. The liberty to have fun, to spend money, and above all to drink to your heart's content! For, ever since the Volsted Act had come into force on October 19, 1919, the United States had been dry. Bootleggers and gangsters held violent sway. The crime rate soared. The name of Al Capone was on everyone's lips. Opinions were polarized by the Sacco and Vanzetti case. To escape from all these vexations, wealthy Americans took to crossing the Atlantic more and more frequently; and, whenever they could, they did so on the ships of the French Line.

Those were the most profitable years for the French Line's New York service. The best year of all was 1928, with a turnover of 560 million francs and a total of 90,000 passengers carried – almost as many as during the period of mass immigration. All this was mainly due to one exceptional ship, which entered service in 1927. John Dal Piaz, the President of the French Line, was quite clear about one thing: nothing was too good for his passengers. On boarding the ship, the traveler must feel at once that he or she was already in France. The bar must be well stocked with whiskey, fine French wines and champagnes. The cuisine must be exquisite, the comfort total, the decor sumptuous and the very notion of boredom unthinkable. The new liner, John Dal Piaz's brain-child, was to be an ambassador for French creativity and French know-how. Her name was *Île-de-France*. Built at a cost of 220 million francs, she was 242 meters (794 feet) long and 28 meters (92 feet) wide, and could carry 673 passengers in first class, 400 in second, and 496 in third, at an average speed of 23 knots. Built at Penhoët, the *Île-de-France* was scheduled to begin her first crossing on June 22, 1927.

One month earlier, on May 21, an American aviator landed at Le Bourget airport near Paris, where he was acclaimed by a crowd of 300,000 people. This hero, whose name was Charles A. Lindbergh, had achieved the first solo crossing of the Atlantic by airplane, covering a distance of 5,809 kilometers or 3,628 miles in a nonstop flight of 33 hours 29 minutes. The intrepid aviator became a living legend.

The directors of the French Line may have applauded Lindbergh's exploit, but their attention was absorbed by the imminent debut of the *Île-de-France*, which was due for dock trials at Saint-Nazaire a week later. On the appointed day the engineers ran the last static test of the ship's engines. The engines were started and suddenly the great ship snapped her chains and steamed the length of the dock basin, gathering speed. Disaster seemed inevitable, when, as if by a miracle, the dock gate swung open. Alone on the bridge, Captain Blancart grasped the wheel and took personal charge of the dangerous maneuver. It was a narrow scrape, but the ocean giant stayed clear of the sides of the narrow channel and came to a halt, undamaged. People said that the *Île-de-France* was a lucky ship right from the start. Throughout a long career, that luck never deserted her.

A few days later, the *Île-de-France* made a triumphal entry into her future home port of Le Havre. She made her first Atlantic crossing at an average speed of 22.81 knots, and New York welcomed her with all the honors due to her rank. As she passed the Statue of Liberty a fleet of tugboats and private yachts escorted her to her berth on the North River. Sirens and foghorns sounded on all sides, and fireboats sent up lofty plumes of water. New York was overjoyed. However, the Federal authorities were not best pleased when they realized that New Yorkers were boarding this dazzling vessel – "the Rue de la Paix of the Atlantic" – and reeling back down the gangplank at midnight.

The *Île-de-France* was French territory; U.S. law did not apply there, and those Americans who were in the know took advantage of her visits to New York to go on board for a drink. At the height of Prohibition this was unacceptable, not to say outrageous. The Congress voted a special law, the Daugherty Act, which laid down that, from that day forward, not only was there to be no alcoholic liquor on any part of United States territory, but no alcohol was to be served on board any ship, whatever the nationality, within U.S. territorial waters.

The French Line protested at once, on the grounds that it was impossible for the company to implement any such measure, since the withdrawal of a French seaman's daily wine ration was deemed to be a punishment under French maritime law. After initially digging their heels in, the Feds gave way in the end. The *Île-de-France* was given permission to dock with her *vin ordinaire* tanks full, on condition that they be placed under seal by the U.S. Department of the Treasury during the ship's stay in New York, and that wine be issued to the crew under the supervision of a Prohibition agent. Despite the best efforts of the Treasury Department, this was the heyday of the *Île-de-France*. To keep the ball rolling, the French Line organized some memorable events. On August 23, 1928 it became the first shipping line in the world to catapult a seaplane from the after deck of a ship (the *Île-de-France*, of course), thus clipping about twenty hours from the time taken by mail to travel between New York and Paris.

The success of the *Île-de-France* was unclouded. Following the example of Maurice Chevalier, who sailed away on October 9, 1928 to find fame and fortune in Hollywood, everyone who was anyone booked a passage on the *Île-de-France*, enjoyed a game of deck tennis before relaxing at the bridge table and danced the foxtrot in a setting worthy of the 1925 Art Déco exhibition. From Georges Carpentier to Gloria Swanson, all the stars of the moment were to be seen rubbing shoulders with the wealthiest people in America. And so, when the liner sailed from New York on October 20, 1929, one first-class passenger in every three was accompanied by a valet, a lady's maid, or a governess. Millionaires and hired help alike would remember that voyage for the rest of their lives.

For the first three days and nights of the crossing, the atmosphere on board was as festive as ever. On the afternoon of the fourth day, October 24, 1929, some alarming news spread along the liner's passageways and into the lounges. One after another, in rapid succession, men discreetly left their tables and gathered in the ship's

Maurice Chevalier and Lucienne Boyer on board the *Île-de-France*, 1950.

hall, with drawn faces, around the blackboard on which the Compagnie de Saint-Phalle posted the latest prices from the world's main stock markets. Incredulous and – worse – helpless, gentlemen in stiff collars watched the collapse of Wall Street, and of their own personal fortunes, played out in real time. On arrival in Le Havre, many were ruined, with no money left to pay off their valets, their lady's-maids or their governesses.

The Great Crash of 1929 thinned out the passenger lists considerably. Freight volumes also decreased, and profits took an equally spectacular dive. The French Line, which had just started a considerable fleet building program (to include, notably, two mixed freight and passenger liners, the *Lafayette* and the *Champlain*), tried to back out of laying the keel of the new liner specified under the terms of its 1927 agreement with the French State – a vessel larger, more luxurious and faster than the *Île-de-France*. But the government, which by now was the company's principal creditor, needed to keep the French shipyard workers employed. It insisted that the work go ahead. The new ship would inevitably be expensive, but the competition made it necessary: the *Bremen* and the *Europa*, of North German Lloyd, had just successively beaten the speed record held by the *Mauretania* since 1909. In Britain, the White Star Line announced that it would soon be laying the keel of a 60,000-ton liner (which was never built). In Italy, Navigazione Italiana had ordered the *Rex* and the *Conte di Savoia*, each 300 meters (984 feet) long; United States Lines were planning to bring into service the *Manhattan* and the *Washington*; Cunard was looking forward to its two redoubtable *Queens*. Every one of these ships was expected to cross the Atlantic in just five days. To remain competitive, French Lines had to act. And so, on October 29, 1930, Penhoët received an order for an ocean liner, codenamed T.6.

Build a new liner? So be it. But this time it would have to be something really special. T.6 was not just another ship. She would be a work of art, a "floating cathedral." Her length of 313.75 meters (1029 feet) would equal the height of the Eiffel Tower. This would be the most sumptuous, the fastest, the most comfortable, the most elegant, the most refined, the most profitable, the most modern and the most prized of all transatlantic liners. The most expensive, too, since she would cost 811 million francs. In a country that had just lost its President – Paul Doumer, murdered on May 7, 1932, by a Russian Anarchist named Gorgulov – this lavish expenditure on a luxury item inevitably led to fierce controversy. The barrage of criticism spontaneously subsided when, on May 11, 1935, T.6 appeared off Le Havre for the first time, proudly bearing her true name, *Normandie*.
"Those who have built this fast and luxurious vessel have not committed the sin of pride. They have been motivated by the desire that France should be represented in international competition by a vessel worthy of her. The *Normandie* is a faithful image of what our country can achieve." So spoke Henri Cangardel,

President of the French Line, in his address to the Archbishop of Rouen, who had come, as custom dictates, to christen the ship before her first voyage. In reply, Monseigneur de la Villerabel made reassuring noises, but he was no doubt reflecting that everything about the *Normandie* was an incitement to sin in one way or another.

"For the first time," wrote Jacques Baschet in a special number of *L'Illustration* for June 1935, "no expense has been spared in the service of a beautiful idea. For the first time, engineers, architects, decorators, painters, sculptors, have been assembled to participate in an enterprise which verges on the irrational, but which fascinates all those who dream of victory in the domain of beauty."

Cue for the expected torrent of superlatives. "The work is done," Baschet continued. "It exceeds all our hopes. No grander or more stirring image of the vitality of our art, its true riches, its robust health, can possibly be imagined." His fellow-journalist Olivier Quéant took up the theme: "The unconvinced and the thoughtless will find in the *Normandie* a reminder that France is not only the land of arts and luxury, of good food and wine, of fashion and perfume, but also the land of science and technology: a science and a technology that have here secured a victory for our national flag and have set an example to the whole world."

On the maiden voyage of the *Normandie*, Blaise Cendrars preferred the engine room to the social whirl above: "I have seen thirty-ton propeller shafts revolving with a permitted play of two-tenths of a millimeter," wrote the adventurer-poet. "I have just spent my first night on watch in the stokehold. I have seen the oil travel from the tanks to the thirty furnaces, into which it streams in a torrent of fire." And while the poet with the missing hand lurked in the belly of the monster, the 1,261 privileged passengers – including Colette, the sailor and novelist Claude Farrère, and his godmother, the President's wife, Madame Albert Lebrun – were lost in admiration of the first-class dining saloon, designed by Patout and Pacon, a vast space 8.5 meters (28 feet) high and 85 meters (280 feet) long: eleven meters longer than the Gallery of Mirrors at Versailles. Life on board the *Normandie*, in the most sumptuous array of lounges, smoking rooms, and galleries ever seen on shipboard, was all leisure and delight.

While those on board were toying with the prospect of a game of deck tennis, or perhaps shuffleboard, on the sun deck, New York was busily preparing to greet "the greatest . . . ship in the history of the world." An exceptional welcome for an exceptional liner. On the morning of June 5, 1935 thousands of New Yorkers crowded onto Pier 88, the brand-new berth of the French Line, still unfinished despite teams of builders who worked day and night. The day was fine. The sky was blue and cloudless. The early mists had dispersed and the sea was virtually calm. With the Ambrose Channel lightship in view, an airplane overflew the *Normandie*, followed almost at once by a squadron of small monoplanes and biplanes.

On board the French liner the party was in full swing. After leaving Le Havre at 6:25 p.m. on May 29, the *Normandie* had covered the 2,971 nautical miles from Bishop Rock in 4 days, 3 hours, 2 minutes: a record speed of 29.94 knots. The ship was dressed overall, and a hundred-foot blue streamer was hoisted on her foremast. The famous Blue Ribbon was once more French. A flotilla of small craft escorted the great ship as she steamed up the Hudson. There was some surprise that her third funnel did not smoke – and this gave way to admiration when it was learned that the funnel was a dummy, that it was there purely for reasons of aesthetics, to maintain the purity of the *Normandie*'s lines – and that it contained the ship's kennels. The writer Philippe Soupault, who was on board, described the scene with great precision in an article for the *Revue de Paris*: "Hardly had we passed the Statue of Liberty, which looked very small to us, when an immense din broke out. All the boats began tirelessly whistling, blowing, letting out hoots, howls, and hurrahs at every pitch; and tirelessly the enormous voice of the *Normandie* boomed out in reply. This tumult resolved itself into a prodigious symphony with the *Marseillaise* as its leitmotif, blaring from a loudspeaker on an airplane. An almost unbearable crescendo that lasted a whole hour, amplified by the echo from the crowded skyscrapers. The towers of Manhattan hastened to meet us. At every stage in our progress, thousands of hands and heads waved and cheered. The only city square that can be seen from the water, Battery Place, was black

The *Normandie*'s bronze propellers. The two principal propellers each weighed more than twenty-two tons and were almost five meters (more than sixteen feet) in diameter.

with people. On all the rooftops were vociferous, surging crowds, hurling little bits of white paper."

In her all-too-brief career, the *Normandie* made 139 Atlantic crossings and carried some 133,000 passengers: as many as the *Île-de-France*, the *Champlain*, and the *Paris* put together. From the moment of that first triumphant arrival in New York, and despite the maiden voyage on May 24, 1936 of the *Queen Mary* – the flagship of the Cunard White Star Line, which took the Blue Ribbon in August of 1936 and again in August of 1938 – the success of the *Normandie* never faltered. Her best year was 1937, when she carried 37,542 passengers on 36 cross-ings and set a new speed record by averaging 30.89 knots westbound and 31.2 knots eastbound. In 1938 the *Normandie* sailed on a historic cruise to Rio de Janeiro which was such a success it was repeated in the following year. But in the summer of 1939 the storm clouds were gathering.

At 2 p.m. on Wednesday, August 23, 1939 the *Normandie* sailed from Le Havre. She was never to see her home port again. During the night a dispatch came through on the teleprinter announcing the nonaggression pact between Hitler and Stalin. The *Normandie* berthed at Pier 88 in New York on August 28, 1939. The *Bremen*, belonging to North German Lloyd, put in at the neighboring pier twelve hours later and sailed the next day without taking on passengers. The *Normandie*, which was also due to sail that day, received orders to stay put.

On September 1, the forces of the Third Reich invaded Poland. On September 3, war was declared, and the *Île-de-France*, with 3,000 Americans on board, was the last vessel to leave Europe for the United States. At the same time, off the Irish coast, a German U-boat torpedoed the British liner *Athenia* without warning, causing more than 300 civilian fatalities.

The *Queen Mary* soon joined the *Normandie* in New York, berthing at Pier 92. A few months later Cunard's most recent liner, the *Queen Elizabeth*, made her maiden crossing and also berthed at Pier 92. She had left Britain in great secrecy, without sea trials, and without her full crew. On March 29, 1940, repainted in gray, the *Queen Mary* sailed for Sydney to be refitted as a troopship. The *Queen Elizabeth* followed a few months later, as did the *Île-de-France*, which reached Singapore on June 30. The *Normandie* remained alone in New York.

On December 7, 1941 the Japanese attack on Pearl Harbor brought the United States into the war. On December 12, the U.S. authorities requisitioned the *Normandie* for conversion into a troopship. Captain Le Huédé and his men were ordered ashore. Overcome by emotion, the French crew sang the *Marseillaise*, as one man, before they walked down the gangway. On January 1, 1942 the liner was renamed *La Fayette*. On January 7, the inventories were completed and the conversion work began. At 2:35 p.m. on February 9, 1942 a workman's blowtorch set fire to the first-class lounge. There was no extinguisher nearby. The fire bucket was accidentally knocked over. The doors to the promenade deck were open, and a strong Northwester fanned the flames. The U.S. Coastguard on duty on the bridge could not find the button for the alarm klaxons. The automatic fire alarm linking the ship with the New York Fire Department had been disconnected on January 13. A policeman on the pier was hailed, by which time the fire had spread to the smoking room and the long gallery. Nobody knew how to shut the fireproof bulkhead that isolated the lounge, or how to work the hose-reels. The American couplings did not fit the French couplings of the fire main, which was not under pressure in any case. The ship was quickly evacuated, and the firemen arrived at last. At around 8 p.m. they announced that the fire had been brought under control. By 8 p.m. the fire was out, but the ship was not saved. Under the weight of the tons of water that had built up in her tanks, the *Normandie* began to list alarmingly. In an hour the list reached 20°. By 11 p.m. it was 40°. At midnight, Admiral Andrews gave the order to abandon ship. At 2:45 a.m., ship's time, the flagship of the French Line heeled over 80° to port, be-tween Pier 88 and Pier 90. The *Normandie* was no more. She lay on the muddy harbor bottom, her two port screws high and dry, her three funnels level with the icy waters of the Hudson.

When World War II ended, the plight of the French Atlantic merchant fleet was catastrophic. The *Lafayette* and the *Paris* had been destroyed by fire in Le Havre in 1938 and 1939, respectively. The *Champlain* had struck a mine off La Pallice in 1940. The *Normandie*, as we have seen, had sunk in New York harbor. The *De Grasse*, scuttled in September 1940, still lay in the waters of the Gironde. Only the *Île-de-France* had come through the war unscathed. She had joined the Free French forces in Singapore in 1940 and had subsequently sailed between Bombay and Suez and between Sydney and San Francisco, transporting more than 300,000 military personnel; for this, she had been awarded the Croix de Guerre. Demobilized in 1947 and completely refitted, the *Île-de-France* received a hero's welcome on her return to New York on June 30, 1949, after ten years' absence.

The British had been more fortunate: both the *Queen Mary* and the *Queen Elizabeth* were intact. The Americans resumed their transatlantic service with the *America* and the *Washington*, and prepared to launch the *United States*. Designed under conditions of great secrecy, the latter smashed the speed record on her maiden voyage in July 1952 with a crossing time of just 3 days, 12 hours, and 12 minutes.

Against such competition, the French fleet looked decidedly the worse for wear. The *De Grasse*, though now refloated, dated back to 1924; the glorious *Île-de-France* had made her maiden voyage in 1927; and the *Liberté* (formerly North German Lloyd's *Europa*, awarded to France as part of World War II reparations) was more than twenty years old. The company's only new ship was the *Flandre*, which entered service in 1952; but she was no match for her redoubtable rival, the *New Amsterdam*, launched in 1948 by the Holland America

Line. Under its most recent contract with the French State, signed in 1933, the French Line was obliged to replace all its ships on the Le Havre-New York run after twenty-five years' service. But the politicians were starting to ask questions. With increasingly serious competition from air travel, did it make sense to spend 28 billion old francs on a prestigious 50,000-ton liner that could transport 2,000-plus passengers at an average speed of 31 knots? Might it not be better to invest in a pair of more modest vessels that would sail at just 25 knots?

In 1953 the question came before the National Assembly. It was eventually answered three years later, after endless parliamentary debates, constant discussions in cabinet and exhausting, repetitious inter-ministerial meetings: three years of oratorical contests, slanging matches, threats, and promises in the vein that was typical of the Fourth Republic. In this case, it must be said, the doubts and hesitations were to prove justified. For the moment, the French Line was carrying more passengers across the North Atlantic than ever before: over a million in 1956 alone, while freight reached a record of three million tons. Air traffic continued to grow, as it had done ever since 1946, reaching 829,318 passengers in 1956; but, on the eve of the centennial of the North Atlantic passenger sea route, no one would have believed that its days were numbered. With support from the Committee for the Reconstruction of the North Atlantic Fleet and with the blessing of a newly elected President,

René Coty (a native of Le Havre), public opinion swung behind the project, and the politicians were forced to make a decision. After many delays and vicissitudes, the contract to build a single giant Atlantic liner was signed on July 25, 1956 at the headquarters of the French Line. The new ship would be the longest in the world, 315 meters (1033 feet) from stem to stern. She would replace the *Liberté* and the *Île-de-France* in six years' time, and her name would be that of the country for which she stood: *France*.

On that very day in July, 1956 the *Île-de-France* was outward bound for New York when, at 11:30 p.m., Captain Raoul de Baudéan received a distress signal from the Italian liner *Andrea Doria*, which had just collided with the Swedish vessel *Stockholm*, 200 nautical miles from New York. The *Île-de-France* immediately changed course and made for the position of the two ships. This was not her first rescue: she had saved so many lives over the years that she was nicknamed "the Saint Bernard of the seas." On that evening, just after the announcement of her coming replacement, the *Île-de-France* worked miracles, saving from certain death no less than 753 individuals. The next morning, July 26, New York gave the French liner a hero's welcome for the third time in her career. She became the first foreign vessel ever to be given the Gallant Ship Award (and was to receive the title of Chevalier du Mérite Maritime on her return to France). Such was the general emotion that the New York pilots' guild refused to bill the French Line for the ship's pilotage, on the grounds that the remarkable rescue effected by the officers and men of the *Île-de-France* would go down in maritime history, and asked the French people to interpret their gesture as a tribute to a remarkable ship and her heroic crew.

In France, the decision to start work on the new liner seemed to have been taken; but in November 1956 the argument flared up all over again. To the surprise of all concerned, the governmental Commissariat-General for Planning postponed the keel-laying of the *France* to allow an oil tanker to be built first. Six months later, in June 1957, the debate resumed on the floor of the National Assembly. Budgetary constraints meant that the issue was wide open again. The cabinet approved the first down payment on July 25, precisely one year after the building of the *France* had been authorized. Work started on October 7. It took the 1,300 workers at Penhoët three years to assemble the gigantic vessel, with her light metal alloy superstructure in which the use of wood was strictly forbidden. The fate of the *Normandie* was on everyone's mind.

Wednesday, May 11, 1960. More than 100,000 spectators converged on Slipway number 1 of the Penhoët shipyard to see the *France* launched. At the appointed time, the immense tonnage of metal shifted majestically and slid down the wooden ramps coated with paraffin wax. The *France* entered the water at the precise moment when the Air Force band struck up the Marseillaise. On his rostrum, General Charles de Gaulle ended his speech thus: "In this vessel we salute one more of those great achievements, on land, beneath the earth, at sea, and in the air, whereby French technology currently bears witness to the greatness of our country. Today's ceremony adds to the pride that we have in France. And now, may the *France* be completed and go out onto the Ocean, to sail and to serve." The crowds applauded their President, but all eyes were on the new giant of the seas, as long as the Eiffel Tower is high, and as tall as a 26-story building.

There was not a cloud in the sky over Brittany that day. But the first Boeing 707s were already in service, and the threat to the *France* came from the sky. That very afternoon, a fleet of Viscounts, Caravelles, Constellations and DC-4s from Hamburg, Frankfurt, Algiers and Brussels had touched down on the tiny airstrip at Montoir, bringing guests from all over the world. In that year, 1960, more than 2,000,000 travelers (twice as many as in 1957) chose to cross the Atlantic by air. Those who went by sea numbered just over 860,000. The numbers were alarming; but the French Line was still hopeful – as would appear from the conclusion of a report that bears the signature of René Laurent: "On the one hand, a fleet of transatlantic liners that needs to be renewed and rejuvenated by the building of new and generally faster vessels, affording the ultimate in comfort and convenience to passengers in general and to tourist-class passengers in particular; on the other hand, the prospect of an upsurge in travel worldwide, caused by advances in transportation, by an improvement in living standards and by an increase in international exchanges of all kinds. Sea travel will thus be able to maintain a role complementary to that of the airplane, for the benefit of all those who still appreciate a style of life and travel better suited to the natural rhythm of our existence."

Crossing the Bay of Biscay in January 1962, the *France* passed the venerable *Liberté*: the new ship returning from her maiden cruise to the Canaries, the old one bound for Italy and the shipbreakers of La Spezia. It was a moving encounter for Captain Croisile, who had himself formerly commanded the *Liberté*. Earlier, on April 10, 1959, the gallant *Île-de-France*, sold to a Japanese owner, had played a part in the wedding celebrations of Crown Prince Akihito. That was the end of her legendary good luck. Within months, a Japanese movie director whose name has not gone down in history had the incredible idea of sinking the liner – torpedoing her – for the purposes of a movie. A sad fate and a sad end for an exceptional ship.

The *France* made her first appearance in New York harbor on February 8, 1962. Her elegant lines, and her unique funnels, shaped like a Spanish Civil Guard's hat, were a great attraction. Her first few years of operation were commercially successful, and she enjoyed a remarkable reputation for quality of service. The menus on the *France* were sumptuous, and her holds were vast. "*France*, the finest restaurant in the world," was the verdict of Craig Claiborne, restaurant critic of the *New York Times*. But this state of grace was not to last.

In 1968, the "May Revolution" broke out in France. Students were tearing up the paving-stones, and nothing would ever be the same again. The first appearance of the *Queen Elizabeth 2* on the New York run, one year later, did not exactly help. General de Gaulle was still the *France*'s greatest fan, but by the time he died in November 1970, the last of the French transatlantic liners was beyond saving. Her fate was sealed. The passenger figures were disastrous: in 1973, just 132,000 travelers chose to cross the North Atlantic by sea, against more than 13 million by air.

In 1974 the *France* was on her second round-the-world cruise, when the rumors of her decommissioning became impossible to ignore. President Georges Pompidou was just about to make the announcement when he died on April 2. The ensuing respite was brief. During his successful presidential election campaign, Valéry Giscard d'Estaing promised to save the *France*, but then the oil crisis dealt a savage blow to the seafaring world, and the French Line faced a projected loss of 100 million francs. The end was inevitable. On July 9 the administration of Prime Minister Jacques Chirac decided to withdraw the liner's subsidy. The French Line immediately announced that she would be withdrawn from service in October. But her ship's company refused to accept the death-warrant.

At 9:06 p.m. on September 11, 1974 the crew of the *France* stormed the bridge and forced Captain Pettré to anchor in the entrance channel to the port of Le Havre. The next day the 1,269 passengers on board were evacuated. Among them was Marvin Dugro Buttles, the American who had bought the very first ticket for the

France eighteen years earlier, and who was now on his fifty-first Atlantic crossing on board. He was not the only American who refused to accept the death of "their" ship. One of them, Abraham Spanel, paid for the *Saturday Review World* of July 22, 1974 to publish an article, signed by the journal's editor, Horace Sutton, which reveals all the affection that he felt for the *France*, and for France itself: "What? Decommission the *France*? . . . As soon renounce truffles. Stop the flow of champagne. Cut down the chestnut trees. Uproot the Rothschild vineyards. Play the *Marseillaise* in waltz time. Cut Joan of Arc out of the history books. Close the Louvre. Give up eating foie gras. Stop making berets. Dismantle the Eiffel Tower. Blow up the Arc de Triomphe. Dress the Saint-Tropez girls in bathing costumes. Smash all of Maurice Chevalier's records. Burn Zola's books. Put arms on the Vénus de Milo. Wipe the smile off the Mona Lisa. . . Take the *France* off the high seas? You might as well put vinegar in all the perfume bottles. Banish Marc Bohan. Show Givenchy the door. Remove Saint-Laurent's halo. Send Cardin to a desert island. Exile the Existentialists. Send Sartre to Siberia. Put Simone de Beauvoir on the slow boat to oblivion. Forbid the ignition of *crêpes Suzette*. Close Maxim's. Free the imprisoned escargots. Declare frogs' legs to be dangerous. Prohibit shrugging. Declare that César Ritz never existed – along with Brillat-Savarin. Pour turpentine on all the Toulouse-Lautrecs. You might as well ban the baguette. Take the café tables off the sidewalk. Remove April from the Parisian calendar. Drain the Seine. Dye the tricolor flag purple and black. Toss all the bouillabaisse overboard. Take the starch out of the chefs' hats. Declare July 14 a working day. Defoliate the Bois de Boulogne. "What? Toss the *France* on the scrapheap? The *France*? Allons enfants! Everyone to the Barricades! . . . "

The *France* was immobilized in Le Havre harbor channel for thirteen days, until a storm forced the mutineers to shelter in the harbor of Saint-Vaast-la-Hougue. After many days of laborious negotiation, the crew decided to return to Le Havre. On October 9, 1974, the *France* entered her home port. In the evening mist, just under 800 people came out to greet the last of the great French ocean liners. A few weeks later, she went to her berth on Oblivion Wharf, *le quai de l'Oubli*, on the fringes of the industrial section of Le Havre. There she remained for five long years until the Norwegian shipowner Knut Kloster bought her, and she sailed (on August 19, 1979) to do the rounds of the blue Caribbean under the new name of *Norway*.

After one hundred and ten years of shared maritime history, the cities of Le Havre and New York no longer had a maritime link. The North Atlantic passenger service was a thing of the past. That vanished age lives on only in pictures and in words.

Before the First World War

The mail service from Le Havre to New York
was inaugurated in 1864 by the steamer *Washington*. The crossing
took an average of fourteen and a half days.

Before the First World War

54   Le Havre-New York

For the first year, the *Washington* and the *Lafayette*
were the only vessels on the North Atlantic run from Le Havre.
The *Lafayette* was a full-rigged sailing ship, and steam long

remained no more than an auxiliary means of propulsion, used in case of flat calm or contrary winds. Until the turn of the century, there were standing orders that sail was to be used whenever circumstances permitted.

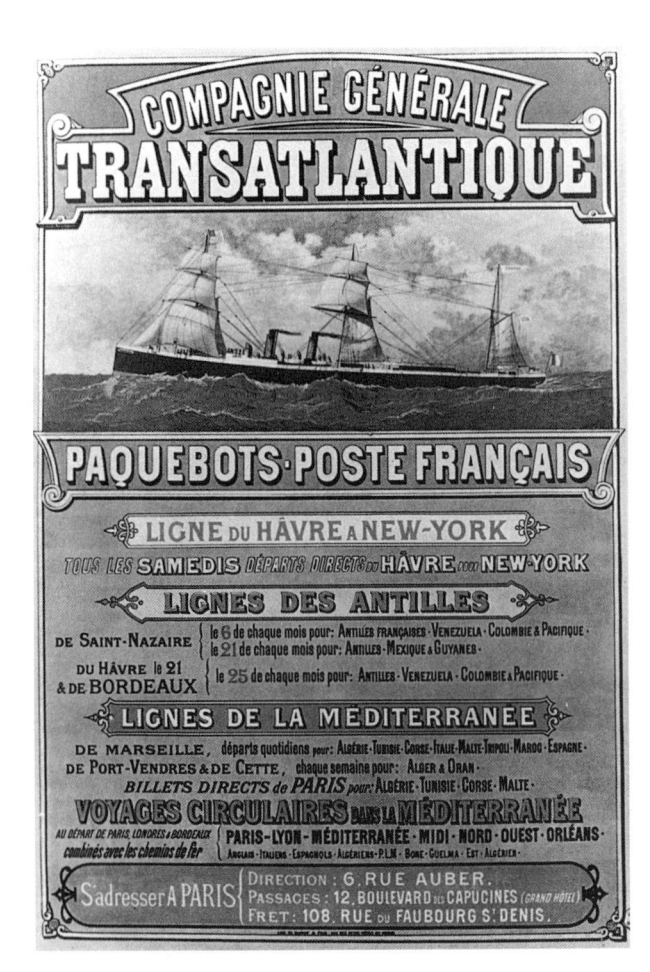

Poster advertising the routes operated by the French Line in the mid 1870's.

Passenger list for *La Normandie*. This was the first French Line ship to have electric lighting and promenade decks.

La Normandie entered service on the North Atlantic run in 1883.
She was the prototype of a long series of similar vessels that ended in 1900 with *La Savoie*.

Before the First World War 59

Passing through the lock at Le Havre. The depth of water being insufficient, it was necessary to trim *La Normandie* by emptying an after ballast tank before she could leave the dock basin.

Cⁱᵉ Gˡᵉ Transatlantique

"LA PROVENCE" 1906

Lancement de "La Provence"

"WASHINGTON" 1863

MENU

POTAGES
OXTAIL ◊ MARIE-STUART

HORS-D'ŒUVRE
PETITES BARQUETTES SÉVIGNÉ

RELEVÉ
SAUMON DE LOIRE A LA DAUMONT

ENTRÉES
FILET DE CHAROLAIS A LA MOSCOVITE
TIMBALE GAULOISE
SORBETS GRANITÉS AU CHAMPAGNE

ROTS
FAISANS TRUFFÉS FLANQUÉS DE CAILLES
MOUSSE DE FOIE GRAS EN BELLE-VUE

LÉGUMES
ASPERGES D'ARGENTEUIL SAUCE RICHE

ENTREMETS
BOMBE GLACÉE "PROVENCE"
ROCHERS DE NOUGAT ◊ RICHELIEU

DESSERTS

◊◊ VINS ◊◊
TISANE PAUL RUINART
CHATEAU SUDUIRANT ◊ CHATEAU-PALMER ◊ CHAMBERTIN
CHAMPAGNE LOUIS RŒDERER

M

A bord de "La Navarre"
21 Mars 1905.

Menu from the dining saloon of *La Navarre*, 1905.
The French Line had neither the biggest nor the fastest ships on the North Atlantic; its trump card was its cuisine.

In 1905, harbor facilities in Le Havre were completed by the building of a rail terminal (Gare Maritime) for the New York service alongside the Bassin du Leurre. Passengers could now embark straight from the boat trains and avoid the perils of transhipment via tender from the quay to the ship offshore.

Le Havre-New York

New York harbor at the turn of the century.

The *Lusitania*. In the race for the Blue Ribbon, awarded for the fastest North Atlantic crossing, the British company Cunard took the lead in 1907 with the *Lusitania* and the *Mauretania*, the two largest liners in the world at that time.

The *Mauretania*, which in 1908 sailed from Liverpool to New York at an average speed of more than 26 knots – a record that was to remain unbeaten for more than twenty years.

The *Titanic*. From the start, the *Olympic* achieved all the commercial success that her owners, the White Star Line, had hoped for. Sadly, her sister ship the *Titanic*, and many of her passengers, was lost on her maiden voyage.

Would-be emigrants underwent rigorous medical examination in order to comply with the draconian provisions laid down by the U.S. Immigration Service.

Before the First World War

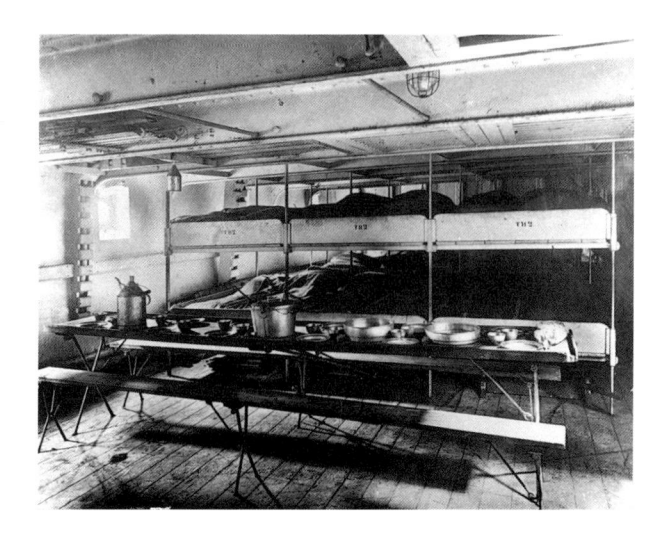

Emigrants traveled in steerage, in dormitories which, in many cases, were segregated by sex. Supplied by the same galleys that fed the crew, the steerage passengers served themselves from communal cooking pots. French Line meals were plentiful and of good quality, and this boosted the company's reputation – as well as its profits – over a period of many years.

New buildings in Le Havre made it possible to handle up to a thousand passengers in transit. Earlier emigrants had had to eat in the vilest cookshacks, and to sleep between-decks on derelict hulks.

To take advantage of the growth in traffic,
the French Line brought into service two ships without first class accommodation.
These "single-class" steamers, the *Chicago* (1908) and the *Rochambeau* (1911),
could carry more than 1,200 emigrants each.

The *France* at Saint-Nazaire. The largest French passenger ship of her day, the *France* entered service with the French Line in 1912. She measured 217 meters (712 feet) long and 23 meters (75 feet) wide.

Before the First World War 71

The *France*, which started operating the week after the *Titanic* tragedy, was a highly successful ship. Her sumptuous decor earned her the nickname of "the Versailles of the Atlantic."

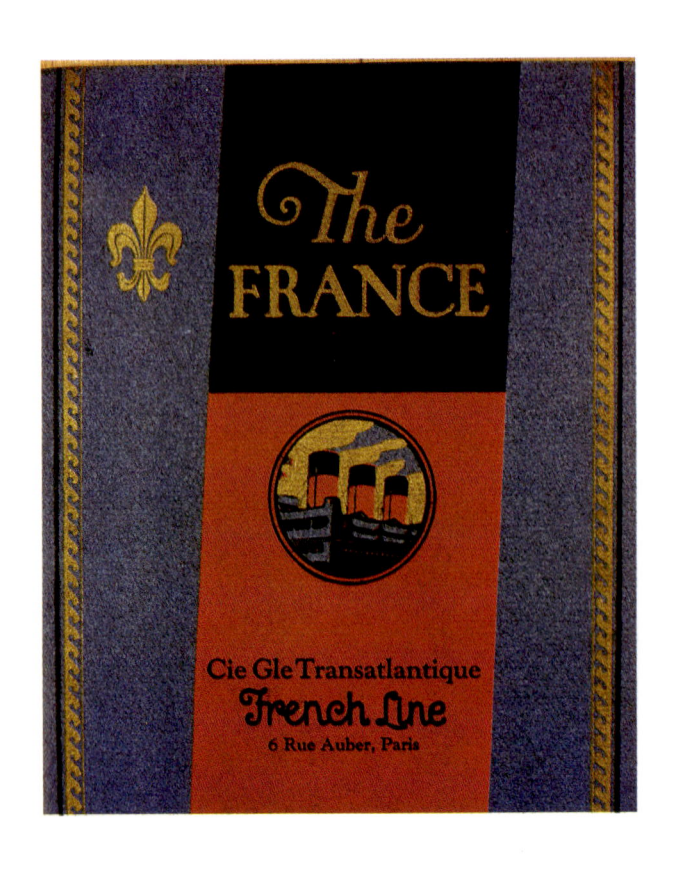

Cover of an advertising brochure.

The dining saloon of the *France* was three decks high,
with a copy of the grand staircase designed by Robert de Cotte for the town
house of the Comte de Toulouse, Grand Admiral of France.

The information bureau on board the *France*.
On this luxurious vessel, the well-being of the passengers was in the hands of a crew of 558.

The third-class smoking room on board the *France*. Including the crew, the ship carried 2,443 persons. Of the 1,885 passengers, 535 were in first class, 442 in second, and 908 in third.

The rotunda of the grand staircase in the first-class section of the *France*.
The wrought ironwork was copied from the staircase in the National Library in Paris.

Designed in the Regency style, the mixed lounge on the *France* contained two paintings by Lacroix de Marseille, dating from 1774.

The engine room of the *France*. Before 1914, the fuel used was coal.
The *France* had 120 furnaces stoked by a complement of 206 firemen and trimmers
working in three watches. She burned 800 tons of coal every day.

Before the First World War 79

Requisitioned early in 1915, painted white with a green stripe and red crosses on her funnels, the *France* spent many months as a hospital ship. In ten round trips, she brought 25,000 wounded men back from the Dardanelles.

Armed with 138-millimeter guns, the *France* arrives in New York on June 4, 1917. She was to make six crossings as a troopship for the American forces, transporting 17,000 men to France and returning 9,000 to the United States.

The *Paris*

The *Paris* was 234 meters (678 feet) long and could carry
561 passengers in first class, 468 in second and 2,210 in third. The crew
numbered 664. In the early 1920's, when the worldwide economic crisis

hit the United States, immigration quotas were cut back, and shipping lines converted the steerage accommodation originally intended for emigrants into quarters for a new breed of passenger: tourist class.

Poster by Albert Sébille for the liner *Paris*. To mark her entry
into service in 1921, the French Line started the first commercial air service
between Le Havre and Le Bourget Airport, Paris.

The three funnels of the *Paris*. On this ship, the safety-conscious French Line experimented with the provision of life jackets for domestic animals.

Grand staircase.

First-class lounge.

A first-class stateroom. The woodwork is in Hungarian oak, grey bird's-eye maple and sycamore or rosewood.

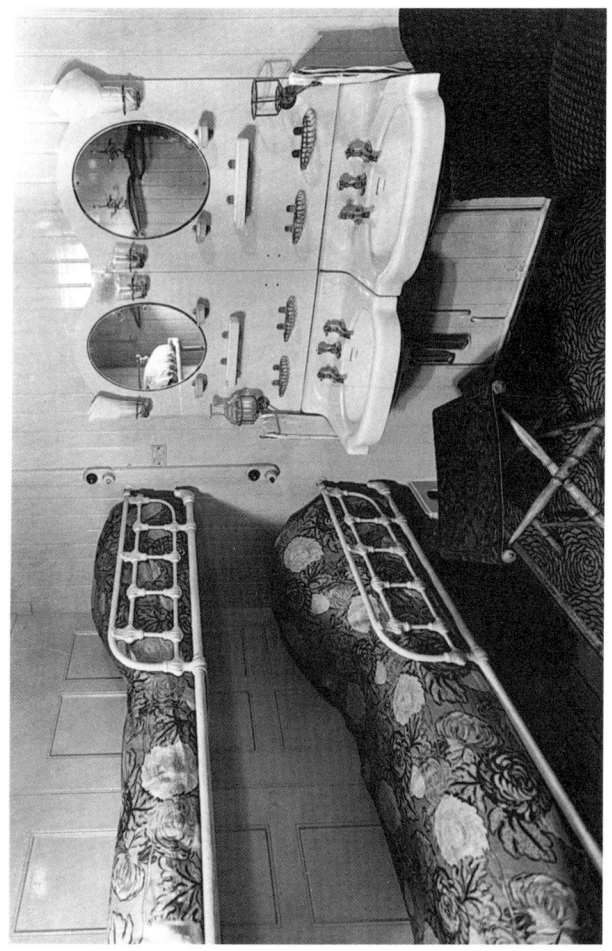

A second-class cabin.

Promenade deck.

Miniature golf. Along with boxing matches on the after deck, this kind of amusement marks the coming of the *style transatlantique* of the early 1920's.

94 Le Havre-New York

Garage.

Engine room.

The *Île-de-France*

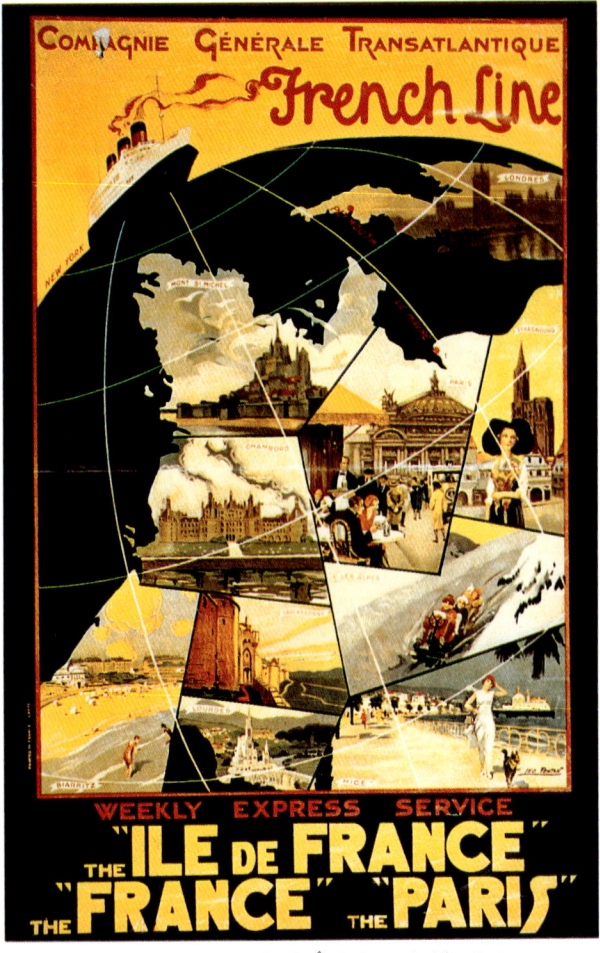

Advance publicity poster for the *Île-de-France*, by Léon Fontan.

The *Île-de-France* docked in Le Havre on June 5, 1927 and sailed for New York on June 22. Her career was to last thirty-two years.

The *Île-de-France* at sea.

The *Île-de-France* arriving in New York. Her design, the quality of her crew, her reliability and regular time-keeping made the *Île-de-France* into the premier vessel on the North Atlantic run.

Grand staircase. The lower level gave access to the chapel, and the upper landing to a tea room. The whole was built of gray Lunel stone and yellow marble.

Tea room. Its immense decorative panel was reflected
in the octagonal mirror on the grand staircase.

First-class dining saloon.

Dance show in the first-class lounge.

Le Havre-New York

Boudoir of Suite 467.

The Île-de-France

Bathroom of Suite 263, an *appartement de grand luxe*.

Passengers playing shuffleboard and boxing match.

Chapel. This was the first chapel ever built on a liner. On other ships, public rooms were converted into places of worship as required.

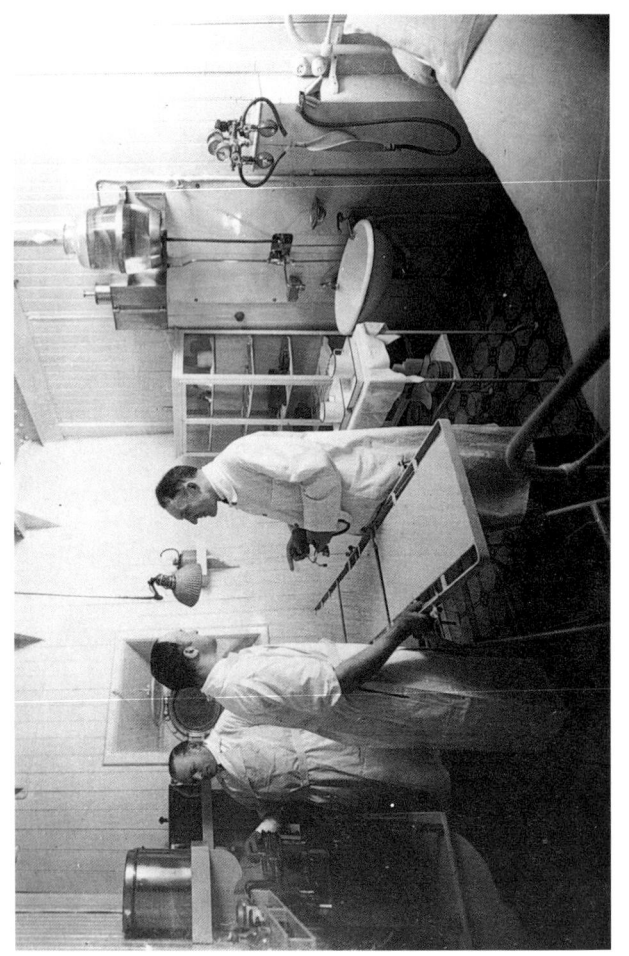

Sick bay.

Printing shop. Here the news received by telegraph from coastal stations was compiled into a daily newspaper, *L'Atlantique*, for the passengers.

In 1928, in order to trim one day off the mail transit time
between France and the United States, the *Île-de-France* was equipped
with a catapult to launch a seaplane.

Poster for the French Line's airmail service.

The 1930's and the *Normandie*

May 17, 1930: the *Lafayette* sails for New York on her maiden crossing. A relatively small vessel, 184 meters (604 feet) long and 25 meters (82 feet) wide, the *Lafayette* was nevertheless the largest French liner ever to rely on diesel propulsion.

The 1930's and the *Normandie* 117

Soirée on the promenade deck of a liner in the 1930's.

An automobile being loaded.

The 1930's and the *Normandie*

Begun in 1931, the *Normandie* was then the largest ship ever built.

The *Normandie* sailing from Le Havre. She entered service on the Le Havre-New York run on May 29, 1935.

French Line poster for the Paris, the *Lafayette* and the *Champlain*.

The 1930's and the *Normandie*

Poster for the *Normandie*.

The smoking-room staircase, which formed the end of an uninterrupted vista 110 meters (361 feet) long.

Dancers in the first-class lounge. This contained a carpet weighing nearly 1,000 pounds, which was rolled back every evening to uncover the dance floor.

Dining saloon. Longer than the Gallery of Mirrors at Versailles, and decorated with giant mural appliques by René Lalique, the dining saloon was equipped (for the first time on any liner) with an air-conditioning system.

The 1930's and the *Normandie*

Wine waiter in the *Normandie*'s wine cellar. In Le Havre, the French Line had built wine and spirit stores with a capacity of 35,000 hectolitres (nearly a million US gallons). The same stores were also used to mature the finest vintages.

Drawing room and bedroom in the Alençon Suite. Ten suites opened off the main deck.

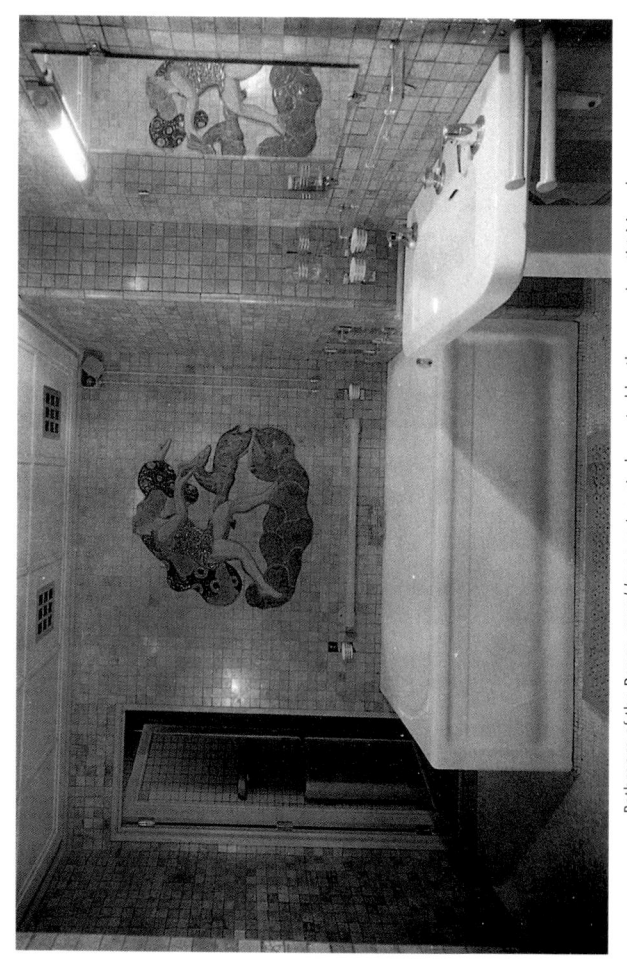

Bathroom of the Rouen *grand luxe* apartment, decorated by the ceramic artist Mayodon. Marlene Dietrich occupied this apartment in 1938.

The Fécamp *cabinet de luxe*, designed by Follot.

The 1930's and the *Normandie*

A first-class stateroom.

Gymnasium.

The 1930's and the *Normandie*

Swimming pool.

The 1930's and the *Normandie*

Poolside bar.

Tennis court on the sun deck. In the background, the skyscrapers of New York City.

The 1930's and the *Normandie* 137

Ship's kennels. These were housed inside the third funnel, which had no other function.

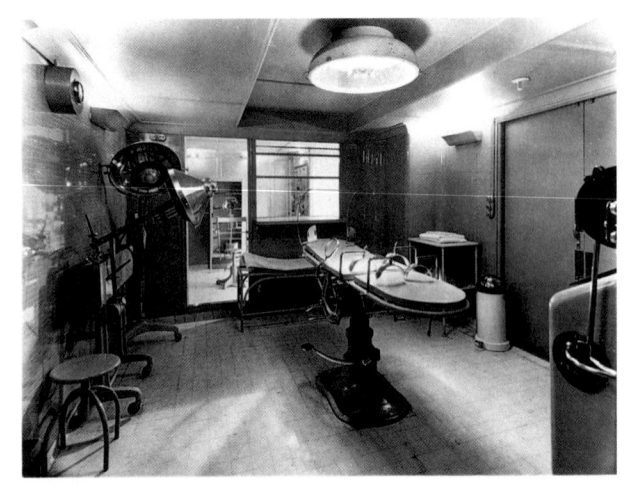

Operating room and crew's mess

Crew's quarters.

Two officers checking the head. There were 21 engineer officers and 21 assistants, supervising an engine-room and stokehold crew of 184 men.

Junior engineer officer at the engine-room telegraph.

Front page of the French Line's daily paper, *L'Atlantique*:
"Maiden Voyage of the *Normandie*."

The *Normandie* arrives in New York.
Without undue pressure on her engines, she took the Blue Ribbon
on her very first crossing.

Pier 88 in New York, first used by the *Normandie* on her maiden voyage in 1935. The legendary Pier 57, which was too short, now fell into disuse.

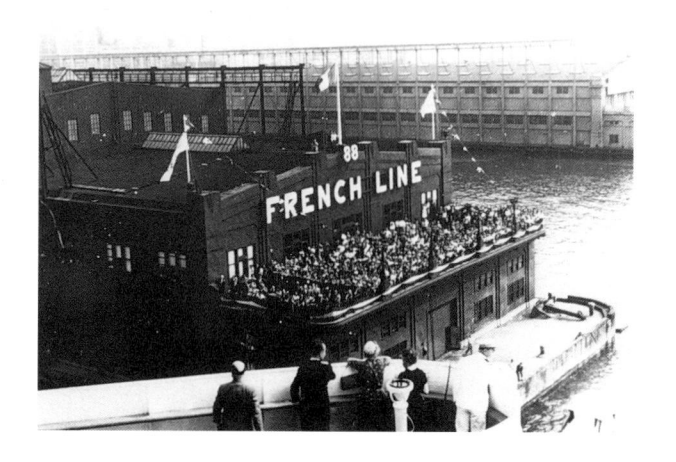

The *Normandie* arriving in New York for the first time. Thirty thousand
people had gathered on the lawns of Battery Park, and thousands of others along
the Manhattan, Brooklyn and Staten Island waterfronts to watch her arrive.

The *Normandie* berths at Pier 88 for the first time. Manhattan celebrated her arrival for five days on end. Two thousand guests were invited to an event at City Hall and two magnificent parties were held at the Waldorf-Astoria.

LOFTS TO LET
PICARD MOTORS
Ford
SALES-SERVICE
PARTS
USED CARS
DAY AND NIGHT
D TRUCKS, All Makes
RESTAURA

Poster for the *Normandie,* by Sébille.

The *Normandie* in New York.

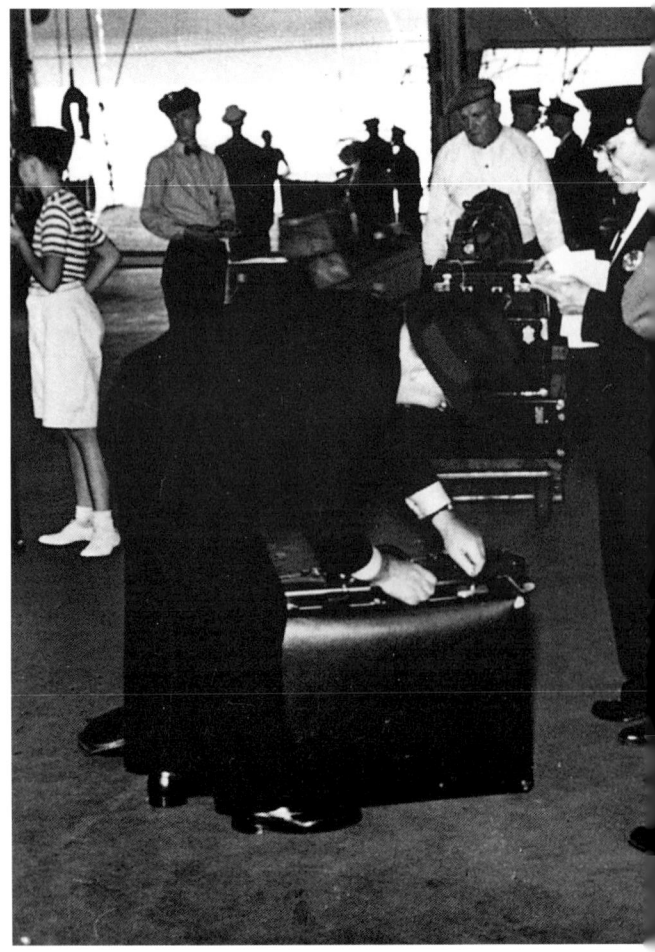

Passengers in the terminal building on Pier 88, New York.

The 1930's and the *Normandie*

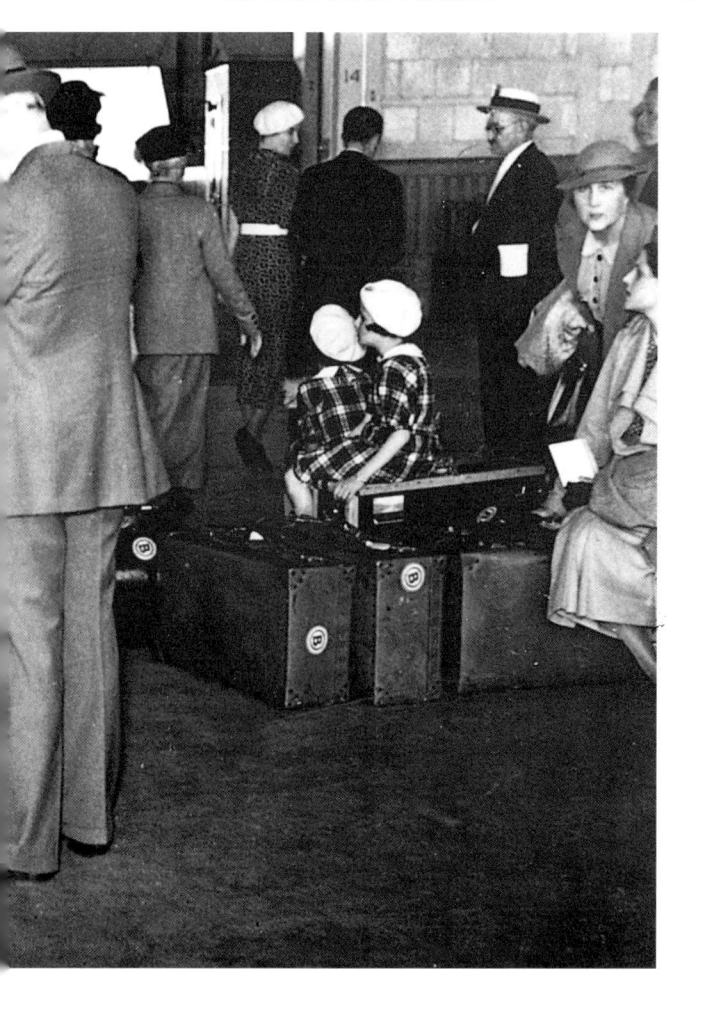

The *Normandie* in New York.

New York harbor in March 1937. From bottom to top: *Berengaria, Georgic, Normandie, Rex, Europa.*

154   Le Havre-New York

Porters at pier 88 in New York.

The 1930's and the *Normandie* 155

Baggage labels.

The *Normandie* escorted by a crowd of small boats
as she sailed from New York for the first time.

The 1930's and the *Normandie*

The *Normandie* steaming down the Hudson.

The 1930's and the *Normandie*

The *Normandie* off Manhattan.

Crew members of the *Île-de-France* who joined the Free French forces during World War II. At the end of April 1940, the French authorities decided to use the ship to transport Indochinese workers to France. En route for Indochina, and after the fall of France, the ship was seized by the British. A number of officers and crewmen signed on to fight the war on the Allied side.

The 1930's and the *Normandie*

The after deck of the *Île-de-France* during World War II.
The public rooms had been converted into dormitories, and extra berths had been installed in the cabins, so that the ship could convey up to 7,000 soldiers.

Under British Admiralty command, the *Île-de-France* transported Australian, New Zealand, Indian, South African and Canadian troops.

The 1930's and the *Normandie*

In July 1942, the passenger-carrying capacity of the *Île-de-France* was increased to 10,500. The interior of the ship was completely stripped, with the exception of the chapel.

Canadian troops homeward bound at the end of World War II. The *Ile-de-France* was awarded the Croix de Guerre for transporting 455,000 men across all the world's oceans.

The *Normandie* on fire in New York on February 9, 1942.
While the liner was being converted for use as a troopship, a workman's blowtorch set fire to the first-class lounge.

Flames destroy the grand staircase of the *Normandie*.

After the fire, the *Normandie* lies on her side between Piers 88 and 90.

The 1930's and the *Normandie*

After the Second World War and the *France*

Painted gray and stripped of all her sumptuous fittings,
the *Île-de-France* was handed back to the French Line in 1947. It was necessary
to modernize her look, recondition her engines and completely renew her
electrical equipment. The internal spaces were redesigned to cut down the first
class accommodation and expand the tourist class. Celebrated artists and
designers were brought in to provide the decor.

Poster for the French Line by Paul Collin.

The *Andrea Doria* after her collision with the liner *Stockholm*, on July 25, 1956. Passengers from the *Andrea Doria*, rescued by the *Île-de-France*, arriving in New York.

Poster by Paul Collin, 1950. The German liner *Europa* was awarded to France as part of war reparations and renamed *Liberté*. Renovated and modernized, she arrived in New York on August 23, 1950.

The *France* under construction at Chantiers de l'Atlantique, Saint-Nazaire.

After the Second World War and the *France*

The *France* was launched at the Saint-Nazaire shipyard on May 11, 1960.

The *France* on the Hudson River.
She made her first Atlantic crossing in February 1962.

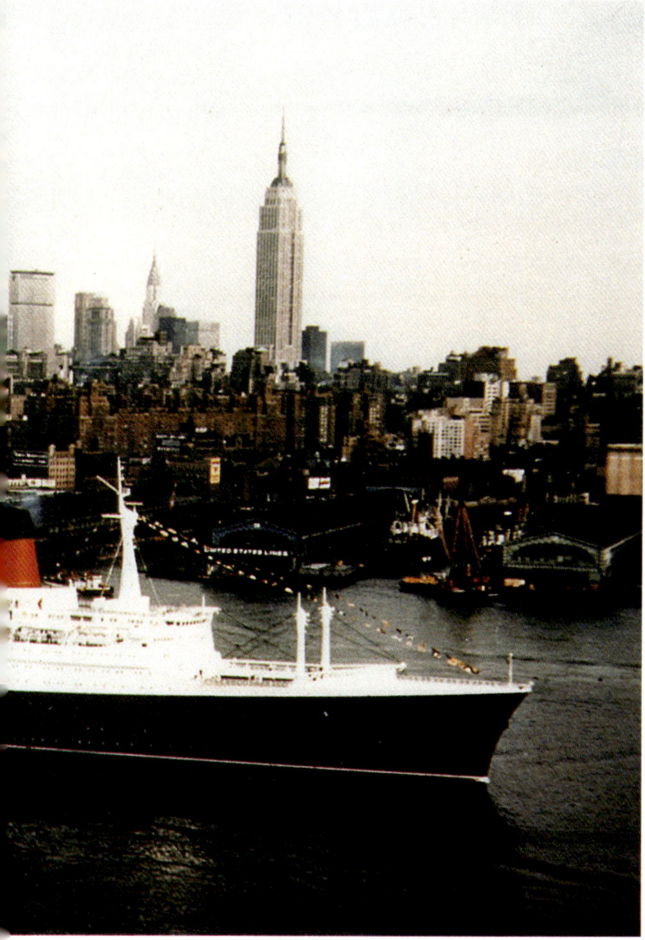

Strollers on the terrace of Pier 88, Manhattan.

After the Second World War and the *France*

The *France* eases in alongside Pier 88, Manhattan.

Poster for the *France*.

The top deck of the *France*.

First-class lounge.

After the Second World War and the *France*

First-class smoking room.

Chambord dining saloon.

Île-de-France suite, with an area of 77 square meters (829 square feet).

After the Second World War and the *France*

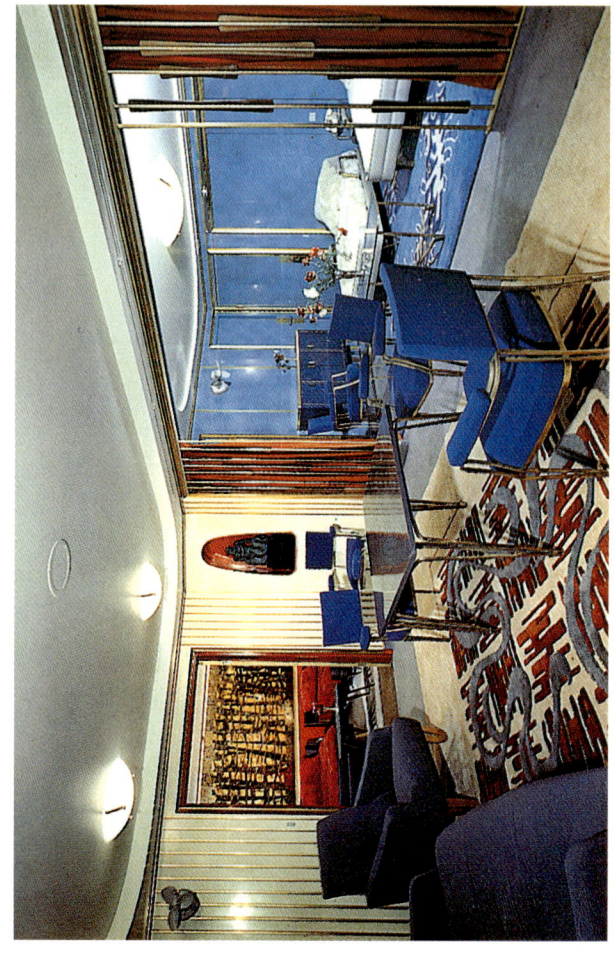

Normandie suite, with an area of 85 square meters (915 square feet).

One of the eight luxury staterooms that opened onto the sun deck, between the two funnels.

First-class swimming pool.

192 Le Havre-New York

Chapel, relatively small in size. The grand theater was used for Sunday Mass.

After the Second World War and the *France* 193

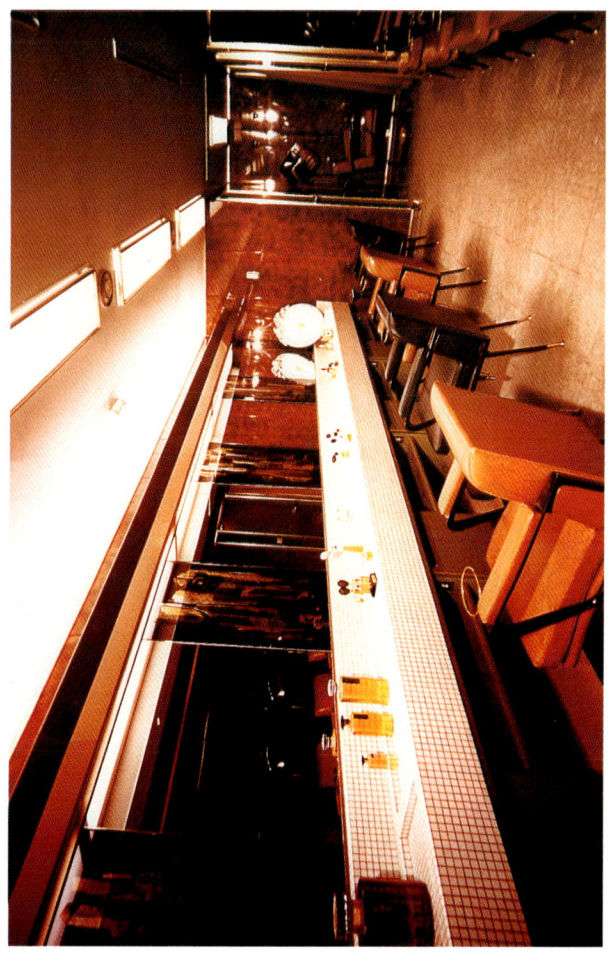

Tourist-class hairdressing salon.

Grand theater, with an area of 3,000 square meters (32,000 square feet).

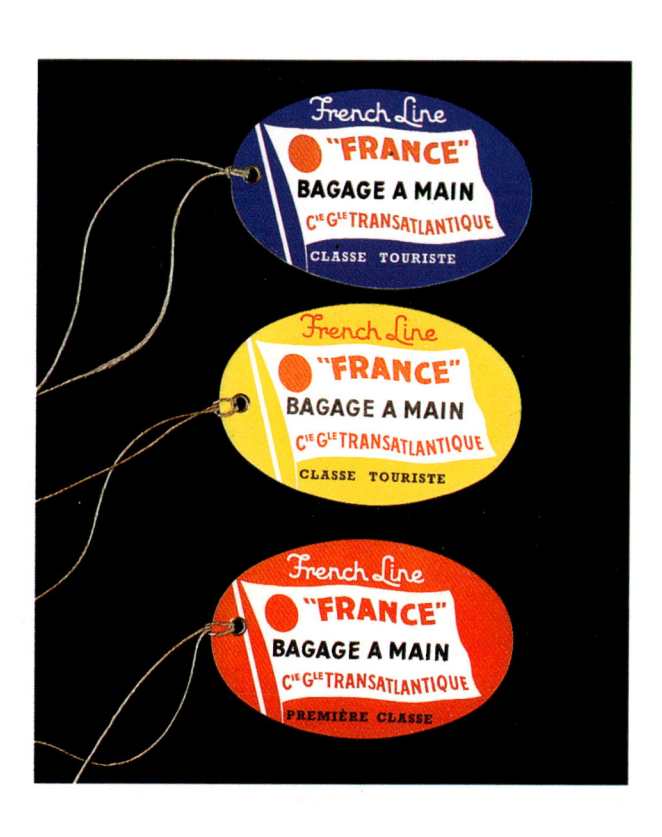

Baggage labels.

Quel pari fou que ce premier Tour du Monde en 88 jours,
pour rappeler le voyage de Philéas Fogg, un siècle plus tôt !

Advertisement for the 88-day world cruise offered
by the *France* in 1972. Like most of the big liners, the *France* was withdrawn
from the Le Havre-New York run in 1974.

The *France* calls at Tahiti in the 1970's.

POCKET ARCHIVES
HAZAN

1 - *Alfred Hitchcock*,
   by Serge Kaganski
2 - *Fernando Pessoa*,
   by Maria José de Lancastre
   et Antonio Tabucchi
3 - *The Spanish Civil War*,
   by Abel Paz
4 - *New York in the 1930s*,
   by Samuel Fuller
5 - *Heartfield versus Hitler*,
   by John Willett
6 - *Architecture and Utopia*,
   by Franco Borsi
7 - *Le Havre-New York*,
   by Christian Clères
8 - *Erik Satie*,
   by Ornella Volta
9 - *The French Resistance, 1940-1944*,
   by Raymond Aubrac